Nineteen Scriptures to Change Your Life Forever

My Life Verses

Matthew Robert Payne

This book is copyrighted by Matthew Robert Payne. Copyright © 2018. All rights reserved.

Any part of this book can be photocopied, stored, or shared with anyone for the purposes of encouraging people. You are free to quote this book, use whole chapters of this book on blog posts, or use this book for any reason if it is to spread the message of Jesus with this world. No consent from the author is required of you.

Please visit http://personal-prophecy-today.com to sow into Matthew's writing ministry, to request a personal prophecy or life coaching, or to contact him.

Cover designed by akira007 at fiverr.com

Edited by Lisa Thompson at www.writebylisa.com You can email Lisa at writebylisa@gmail.com for your editing needs.

All scripture is taken from the New King James Version unless otherwise noted. Copyright © 1982 by Thomas Nelson, Inc. Used by permission. All rights reserved.

All scripture quotations marked (NLT) are taken from the Holy Bible, New Living Translation, copyright ©1996, 2004, 2007, 2013, 2015 by Tyndale House Foundation. Used by permission of Tyndale House Publishers, Inc., Carol Stream, Illinois 60188. All rights reserved.

The opinions expressed by the author are not necessarily those of Christian Book Publishing USA.

Published by Christian Book Publishing USA.

Christian Book Publishing USA is committed to excellence in the publishing industry. Book design Copyright © 2018 by Christian Book Publishing USA. All rights reserved.

Paperback: 978-1-68411-575-4

Dedication

To Mary:

I want to dedicate this book to my beloved friend, Mary. She takes the time to read all of my books and is a great support to me even though she lives overseas. Mary does not judge me when I share my struggles with her and is very positive about my life and my future in God.

Every person should have a loving and supportive friend like Mary in their life. She knows me very well, and her prayers keep me going.

Acknowledgments

Jesus:

I want to thank you for being my lifelong friend and for never deserting me, no matter how dark my life became.

Holy Spirit:

I want to thank you for leading and teaching me. You are a great teacher, better than I could ever be. I want to thank you for speaking through me and being my co-author. I am learning to know you more and more each year.

Father:

Thank you for loving me and entrusting me with this life that I am living. Thank you for revealing my purpose to me and leading me toward accomplishing it. Thank you so much for your Son, Jesus. Thank you for everything that you have done in my life.

Lisa Thompson:

I want to give special thanks to Lisa for editing this book of mine. You take my simple words and transform them to make me seem smarter than I really am. If you have any editing needs, Lisa can be contacted at writebylisa@gmail.com

Nicola:

I want to thank Nicola for being part of my team as a proofreader. I want to thank you for all the work that you did with this book to polish and improve it.

Bill Vincent:

I want to thank you, Bill, for publishing my book. You can contact Revival Waves of Glory Books & Publishing if you need any books published.

Friends:

I want to thank Lisa, Nicola, Mary, Wendy, Laura, David Joseph, and Michael Van Vlymen for your friendship and how you have impacted my life.

Mom and Dad:

I want to thank my mother and father for all the love that they have given me. I am a product of your love.

Readers and ministry supporters:

I want to thank the readers of my books and my ministry supporters for the funds that you have given me to publish books. I live to educate people, and I thank both my readers and the supporters of my ministry because you make life worth living.

A Note from My Editor

Dear Reader,

I love the Word of God and have memorized many verses over my lifetime. When Matthew told me about this book, I was thrilled that he chose to write on a subject so near and dear to my heart.

I was so encouraged as I went through the editing process. Matthew has selected a wide range of amazing passages from both the Old and New Testament. This book will be a handy reference to encourage people with some extremely powerful verses.

As you read, take the time to meditate on each scripture. Allow the Lord to minister to your heart and bring you the healing and hope that these verses inspire.

If you have any writing or editing needs, I am happy to help. You can learn more about me at my website at www.writebylisa.com or reach me via email at writebylisa@gmail.com

God bless you all!

Lisa

P.S. My favorite passage that Matthew has shared is Psalm 1. I love the profound simplicity and the deep wisdom of this chapter.

Table of Contents

Dedication 3
Acknowledgments 4
A Note from My Editor 6
Chapter 1 8
Chapter 2 12
Chapter 3 16
Chapter 4 20
Chapter 5 25
Chapter 6 30
Chapter 7 33
Chapter 8 37
Chapter 9 41
Chapter 10 45
Chapter 11 49
Chapter 12 54
Chapter 13 58
Chapter 14 62
Chapter 15 66
Chapter 16 70
Chapter 17 73
Chapter 18 78
Chapter 19 83
Closing Thoughts 86
I'd love to hear from you 89
How to Sponsor a Book Project 90
Other Books by Matthew Robert Payne 91
About Matthew Robert Payne 94

Chapter 1

Psalm 1:1–3

"Blessed is the man who walks not in the counsel of the ungodly, nor stands in the path of sinners, nor sits in the seat of the scornful; but his delight is in the law of the Lord, and in His law he meditates day and night. He shall be like a tree planted by the rivers of water, that brings forth its fruit in its season, whose leaf also shall not wither; and whatever he does shall prosper."

"Blessed is the man who walks not in the counsel of the ungodly." You might have friends that are gossiping with wrong spirits or who are involved in certain sins and terrible behavior. If you want to obey this verse, you will have to separate yourself and walk away from them. If that means you lose all your friends, so be it.

Obeying this verse means you don't walk with Christians that are doing ungodly things. You should avoid Christians who are involved in sexual sin outside of marriage. If you have friends like that (and I did), you need to stay away from them.

"Nor stands in the path of sinners." You need to get away from people who are an obstruction to others coming to the saving grace of Jesus. If someone's life is a poor testimony that stops people from being saved, you need to stop spending time with those people. You need to transform yourself so that you're helping—not hindering—people from being saved.

"Nor sits in the seat of the scornful." If you spend time with people who have religious spirits, who are mockers, who make fun of authority, and who have issues with leadership and those in ministry, you need to get away. Stay away from those sorts of people, these mockers. I had a group of those friends, and the Lord used this verse to convict me to move away and stop hanging around them.

"But his delight is in the law of the Lord, and in his law he meditates day and night." This person meditates and spends his time in the Word of God. If you want to apply the promises of God to your life, you will need to move away from those negative influences and spend time in the Word of God. You don't necessarily have to read the Word of God every day, but the Word of God should guide your life.

You can actually chew on a verse for years and years in a certain type of meditation. I've heard meditation compared to how a cow chews on its cud. Although it's rather disgusting, this description drives the point home. The cow chews the cud and then regurgitates it back up. It then keeps chewing and regurgitating until the cud is finally digested. This is how we should be when it comes to meditating. Keep mulling the verses over and over in your mind, thinking about them throughout the day. Continue this process for weeks or even months or years. In this way, these verses will become part of you, and you will live them out to their fullest extent.

The verse can be part of your subconscious and your conscious mind. You can be thinking about the verse, meditating on it, and chewing on it to pull every bit of goodness from the verse. As I described in the last paragraph, that's what David means when he talks about meditating on the Word day and night. Your whole life is fashioned by the Word of God. I have meditated on this passage for twenty years.

"He shall be like a tree planted by the rivers of water." The rivers of water are symbolic of the Holy Spirit. The tree might be an oak tree planted by the rivers of water. The Holy Spirit is feeding the root system of that tree. The tree has abundant fruit and leaves and can sustain birds and different animals eating its fruit. Even humans eat of the fruit and relax under its shade.

You become like this righteous holy tree that brings forth its fruit in season whose leaf does not wither. You bring forth the fruit of the Spirit and other godly attributes. The fruit of the Spirit helps you deal with people through love, joy, peace, patience, goodness, kindness, gentleness, faithfulness, and self-control. (See Galatians 5:22–23.) Other ways to help people include monetary help, spending time with someone, and compassion.

These qualities can help people so much. They include your time, your understanding, your listening ability, your healing ability, your gift of prophecy, and more. These are all part of the fruit that comes from your life. You're this righteous tree who bears fruit. I do that every month when I produce a new book as a writer. Every month, new readers read a book that I've written and produced. A source of fruit constantly comes from my life.

Every week, someone emails me, who says that they've read a number of my books. Their lives have been transformed and gone to another level from reading my books. My books are hard to put down. This is fruit that comes from my life.

"Whose leaf also shall not wither." That means that when the times of drought come, you're able to endure. The tree is always prospering and healthy with green leaves. It isn't affected by drought or hard seasons.

"Whatever he does shall prosper." This is a key to the favor of God. I meditated on this verse for many years before the favor of

God came into my life. When the favor of God comes upon your life, you see success at whatever you turn your hands to. I started a ministry, requesting people to pay for prophecies and different services from my website, and the Lord has used it to bless me. Whatever I did prospered, and many people have enjoyed my books and have even seen fit to send me as much as three thousand dollars to finance and publish a new book.

When your life measures up to this passage, when you get away from those wrong people, when you stop hanging around the wrong crowd, when you stop hanging around sinners but delight in the law of God, in the Bible, meditating on it, then you will become a prosperous tree, watered by the Holy Spirit. Everything you do is directed by the Holy Spirit, who can give you fruit in season. Your leaf will not wither, and whatever you turn your hand to will prosper. Whatever you decide to do, the Lord's favor is upon your life because you're led by the Holy Spirit.

This is one of my favorite verses and is being fulfilled in my life. This verse didn't just apply to King David but is also true in my life. It is one of my life's verses, which is why I wanted to share it with you. When this verse manifests in your life, you will have a radically different life.

Chapter 2

Jeremiah 17:7–8

"Blessed is the man who trusts in the Lord, and whose hope is the Lord. For he shall be like a tree planted by the waters, which spreads out its roots by the river, and will not fear when heat comes; but its leaf will be green, and will not be anxious in the year of drought, nor will cease from yielding fruit."

"Blessed is the man who trusts in the Lord." This person puts their faith in the Lord. This person isn't directed by his own thoughts and his own reasoning but is directed by the Lord God. This person hears from and is directed by the Holy Spirit.

For example, I finished editing a book yesterday, and I came to the conclusion that I need to start writing a new book. The Holy Spirit led me to do a book on my life verses. I sat down at the computer and started typing my favorite verses in a Microsoft Word document. Then the Holy Spirit actually led me to each different verse and brought to remembrance the verses that I really love and stand on. Then I went to Bible Gateway and organized all the verses in the Word document and printed them out. I collected nineteen verses that I put into nineteen chapters in this book. These verses mean so much me. The process was easy, which is how life is when you are directed and led by the Holy Spirit.

I'm led by the Lord. This verse says, "Blessed is the man who trusts in the Lord." We are not only to trust in the Lord but to obey him and be led by him. You can go two ways in this world: man's way and what seems right to your flesh or God's way. Sometimes God's way is counter-cultural.

"Whose hope is in the Lord." When you hope in the Lord, you don't trust in:
- your job
- in finances
- what the paper says
- what the news says or what the media tells you to do or
- having a nice house, clothes, cars, and possessions.

Instead, you place your hope in the Lord himself to be your supplier.

The Lord needs to be the one that promotes, directs, and inspires you. You should not trust in your own mind or your own intellect. Instead, put your hope and your trust in the Lord Jesus through the Holy Spirit.

If you do those two things—trust in the Lord and have your hope focused on him—then the rest of the passage applies to you.

"For he shall be like a tree planted by the waters." Once again, we have a tree, similar to what Psalm 1 mentioned in the first chapter. You become this tree that sustains life. You become this tree that can not only live a satisfying and prosperous life, but you can be full of fruit and feed other people. You become not only prosperous yourself but can give to others and supply the needs and desires of needy people.

"Which spreads out its roots by the river." Those roots go into the river of the Holy Spirit. Can you imagine living your life so that most of your thoughts and actions are led by the Holy Spirit? That's an example of someone whose roots are spread out by the river. The river of God, the Holy Spirit, supplies every action that person takes.

This is an example of being led by the Spirit. The Holy Spirit told me to stay up tonight and do the recordings for this book. These recordings are each ten minutes, and I need to record nineteen of them. So recording tonight will take me just over three hours.

"Who will not fear when the heat comes." This person who is a tree planted by the waters no longer worries about heat. When hard times come, when darkness comes to the world, when times of oppression or trials come, when wilderness experiences come, whatever comes against the Christian church or against you personally, you won't fear because you are being led and directed by God. Your trust is in God; your trust is not in men. You do not fear when the heat comes. When the pressure comes upon you, you won't fear because you're being directed by the Holy Spirit.

Since I started my ministry, I have never wanted for finances to produce a book, which costs me approximately two thousand dollars a month. The Lord brings in money to supply the needs.

"But its leaf will be green." Like Psalm 1 says, you'll always be in a state of healthy growth; you won't have brown leaves or leaves that are dead. If you ever look at nature, you might see green trees by the riverbank, but all the surrounding fields are brown. Those trees stay green because they're fed by the river, but all the rest of the land is barren and brown. You'll be a tree on those river banks, a person who's fulfilled, sustained, and healthy even in the midst of drought.

"Will not be anxious in the year of drought." When hard times come and there is pressure in the Christian community, when trouble comes with all sorts of pressure against you as a Christian, you won't be anxious because you're being sustained and led by the Holy Spirit. Your trust and hope are in the Lord, and you'll have plenty of personal testimonies to carry you and give you faith, testimonies of when God has been your provision, when God has stood up for you, when God has acted on your behalf, and when God has answered your prayers.

"Nor will cease from yielding fruit." You're going to be in a position where you're always producing fruit. Like I said, I produce one book a month; I interact with people on Facebook; and I minister in the church and teach others how to hear from God, how to prophesy, and how to witness to people at prophetic events. My life is full and active with tremendous fruit in my ministry. It is certainly a good ministry to sow into. I live a productive life. This verse, this passage, has been one of my life verses, and I find it very impressive. I encourage you to study this verse along with the surrounding passages.

Like Psalm 1, this verse promises that you will yield fruit, and when hard times come, you will not be affected. It is a great passage to know and to come into agreement with so that it starts to manifest in your life. I often look at leaders like Bill Johnson, Kris Vallotton, Francis Chan, Benny Hinn, Joyce Meyer, and Andrew Wommack, and I see passages like this manifesting in their ministries. It is my prayer that my readers learn to trust the Lord and follow him.

Chapter 3

Proverbs 3:5–10

"Trust in the Lord with all your heart, and lean not on your own understanding; in all your ways acknowledge Him, and He shall direct your paths. Do not be wise in your own eyes; fear the Lord and depart from evil. It will be health to your flesh, and strength to your bones. Honor the Lord with your possessions, and with the first fruits of all your increase; so your barns will be filled with plenty, and your vats will overflow with new wine."

"Trust in the Lord with all your heart, and lean not on your own understanding." This follows on the theme of trusting the Lord. If you haven't heard this description before, this verse is saying to trust in the Lord with all of your spirit and with all of your heart and lean not on your own understanding. It means to lean not on your own mind and what your mind says.

A person has to learn how to be led by the Holy Spirit, how to be directed by the Spirit of God, who speaks to your heart, speaks to the core of you. Many times, the Lord will lead you to do something in your spirit, through your heart. You start to think about it with your mind, and you talk yourself out of it. This is what this verse by Solomon is saying. "Trust in the Lord with all of your heart." Don't just give mental assent to the Lord. Don't say you trust the Lord without doing everything that the Lord directs you to do through your spirit. Don't let your mind talk you out of obeying. That's so important. Being led through your spirit is akin to being led by your intuition or to having a gut feeling about something. We need to be led by those feelings and not thoughts in our minds that contradict those. Understanding this and living your life accordingly is key to a successful Christian life.

"In all in your ways acknowledge Him, and He shall direct your paths." If you listen to the Lord through your intuition and spirit and if you acknowledge that he's directing you, then he will direct all your paths. He will make sure that everything you do works out well. Like I've said before, you won't have brown leaves on your tree, and you'll always bear fruit. Whatever you do will prosper if you trust in the Lord with all your heart and do not lean on your own mind and understanding. This will happen if you acknowledge the Lord in all you do. Give the Lord all the glory in what you do. You can talk about the Lord and express how he has led you and blessed you, and he will continue to direct your path. This is a really important key to not only know but to actually live out.

This is how I live. Every day, my life is directed by the Holy Spirit. Everything I do is directed by the Holy Spirit except when I sin, which is obviously not directed by the Holy Spirit. Most of my life is really directed by the Lord.

A visiting apostle came to our church about ten years ago and said to my father that he had never seen anyone who flowed with the Holy Spirit as much as I did. My father said that he thought I would have a big head if he told me. My mother and I asked him to tell us because he said the apostle said something that would make any father proud. It's true. I'm led in everything I say and do, which is why many people say my books are anointed. Almost everything I have to say is led by the Lord. You can be led by the Lord in this same way.

"Do not be wise in your own eyes; fear the Lord and depart from evil." Do not be wise in your own eyes means that you should not be proud. Don't think you're smart. Understand that you have a lot to learn. Understand that the more you know, the more you need to know. Submit yourself to the Lord and humble yourself under God's mighty hand, and in due time, he'll lift you up (1 Peter 5:6). You need to learn to revere the Lord and depart from evil. You need to stop doing what the enemy tells you to do. You need to respect the Lord and honor and fear him.

"It will be health to your flesh, and strength to your bones." Sin and wrongdoing can have consequences. When you obey and walk uprightly, this verse promises that it will be health to your flesh and strength to your bones. It sounds like the best plan for your health is to fear the Lord and depart from evil. Also, pride can cause disease in your life. You should not be wise in your own eyes.

"Honor the Lord with your possessions, and with the first fruits of your increase." Many people passionately teach against tithing. I always honor the Lord in giving and its part of who I am. I love to give. Every time someone gives me a nontaxable donation, I tithe 10 percent of that. Every time people give me money, these first fruits that come into my ministry, I tithe on them. I give to the Lord.

If you do that, the next verse says, "Your barns will be filled with plenty, and your vats will overflow with new wine." Not only will the Lord prosper you if you honor him with your possessions and with the first fruits of your increase, but he will also make sure that the Holy Spirit is giving you new wine, not only physical wine to drink, but a new wine from the Holy Spirit so that you are inspired and receive revelations from God.

"Your vats will overflow with new winefringes." This means you'll be living in a state of abundance and from a place where you have enough money and enough resources to do everything you need to.

Since the start of my ministry two years ago, I have been pursuing the Lord and doing everything the Lord has told me to do. I've been producing one book a month. I've been directed to do everything I do, and as I obey the Lord, I have written every book that he has asked me to write. Some of my books, such as doing interviews with saints, are controversial and hard to do, but I pursued the Lord, and he made sure that my vats and my barns have overflowed with plenty, and he's giving me the new wine. The Lord is giving me plenty of revelation to share in my books. Some people are just amazed at the revelation that comes from them.

I can say that the fresh revelation that I receive is a result of honoring the Lord financially. So many people have a problem with giving because they give from the wrong spirit. They give grudgingly because they feel like they're forced to give, or they give in order to get back from the Lord because they think they will be blessed tenfold. They just don't have the spirit to bless the Lord and ministries that are serving the Lord.

I have this wonderful giving spirit. I love to give. The Lord certainly supplies me with finances and regularly puts it on the hearts of people to give my ministry money and support me. This passage or scripture is so profound and so deep. I could possibly do a whole book on this series. I hope you learned something from this.

I hope you enjoyed this chapter. The words of this passage are just so rich and full of promise. The Lord really does lead his people and orders their steps. The Lord is trustworthy and quite able to prosper you as you sow into him. You will be blessed when you obey the Lord if you are not wise in your own eyes.

Chapter 4

Isaiah 60:1–6

"Arise, shine; for your light has come! And the glory of the Lord is risen upon you. For behold, the darkness shall cover the earth, and deep darkness the people; but the Lord will arise over you, and His glory will be seen upon you. The Gentiles shall come to your light, and kings to the brightness of your rising. Lift up your eyes all around, and see: They all gather together, they come to you; your sons shall come from afar, and your daughters shall be nursed at your side. Then you shall see and become radiant, and your heart shall swell with joy; because the abundance of the sea shall be turned to you, the wealth of the Gentiles shall come to you. The multitude of camels shall cover your land, the dromedaries of Midian and Ephah; all those from Sheba shall come; they shall bring gold and incense, and they shall proclaim the praises of the Lord."

"Arise, shine for your light has come! And the glory of the Lord is risen upon you." What does that mean? Twenty-five years ago, I was walking down the street in Brisbane, a northern city in Australia, and everyone was staring at me. I wondered if they thought that I had green hair! Was something wrong with me? The whole day, people stared at me. I went into the bathroom to look at myself in the mirror to see if I looked strange. People stared at me and then walked up to me, asking me for the time. I didn't have a watch on, and it was years before mobile phones or cell phones. They could see that I didn't have a watch, and it was pretty silly to ask me for the time. Other people would come up and ask for a light or a smoke. I finally realized that people were just trying to find any reason to talk to me.

I wondered why. Mainly the smokers, people with tattoos, those that seemed to be on the fringes of society back then, were brave enough to come up and ask me a question.

Later that night, I was watching a busker on the street and listening to his music. A guy on a skateboard came up, and he asked, "What is it about you?"

I replied, "What do you mean, 'What is it about you?'"

He said, "What do you believe?"

I answered, "I believe in Jesus. I'm a Christian."

He said, "I'm a Christian, and I believe in Jesus too. But what is it about you?"

I said, "What do you mean?"

He said, "What is it about you?"

I said, "Well, I am Spirit-filled."

He replied, "I'm Spirit-filled too. But what makes you different? What is it about you?"

I was trying to listen to the busker, and I grew impatient with him disturbing me because I wanted to listen. I said, "What do you mean? What is it about me?"

He said, "Your face is glowing. It's like when people put a torch in their mouth. Your whole face is shining, and I want to know how to do that."

I was tired and exhausted from people looking at me all day. I said, "I have no idea how that's happening."

This verse illustrates how others can physically see glory on your face. Sometimes you shine like the sun, and your face just lights up.

One way to tell if the glory can be seen on you is if a baby will stare at you. Babies will be fascinated by you and keep on looking at you. Homeless people will ask you for money. You can be walking down the street, and a homeless person will speak to you, and they won't speak to anyone else. People who need directions will seek you out. Twenty people in front of you might walk past the person, and they didn't stop anyone else. When you come to them, they stop you and ask you for directions. Something in them is saying, "This person will take their time to help me."

Another sign of glory being on you is if a person opens up to you and tells you their whole life story. They will say something like, "I never told anyone this before, but I felt comfortable telling you." If that seems to happen to you, a measure of glory is on your life. This verse is talking about the glory of the Lord coming upon a person. This glory will come upon us. This verse doesn't just refer to the Jews but to the new Israel of God. This glory will come upon certain people in the end times.

"For behold, the darkness shall cover the earth, and deep darkness the people." We certainly know that the world is getting darker, but in spite of this, we can see God's promise in the next verse.

"But the Lord will arise over you, and His glory will be seen upon you." Not only did this happen to me in Brisbane, but it has happened to me other times. Everyone has stopped and stared at me when I've been out shopping. The next time it happened, I went to buy take-out food from a restaurant. About twenty people were lined up, waiting to be served. When I approached the back of the line, one of the servers saw me and said, "Can I help you?" I was aware that I was shining that day, and so she wanted to help because I seemed like an angel to her. I was glowing like an angel.

Because I was aware that I was shining, I said, "No, plenty of people are in front of me that need to be served first. You serve them while I wait my turn."

Everyone turned around to look at me and see who this person was that she wanted to serve. They wanted to know who had such favor on his life. I smiled at them, and they were pleased that I was going to wait. They probably saw the glory of the Lord on me too.

I started a conversation with the young girl in front of me, and we had a nice conversation.

"The Gentiles will come to your light, and kings to the brightness of your rising." Both the glory and the favor of the Lord will come on certain people. If his glory rests on you, people will be attracted to you, and even kings and people in leadership will come to your anointing.

"Lift up your eyes all around, and see: they all gather together, they come to you; your sons shall come from afar, and your daughters shall be nursed at your side." You can become a spiritual father or mother to many people. Others can look up to you as an influence, as a spiritual parent. This is happening to me already, and many people are being mentored and encouraged by my influence on Facebook and by the books that I write.

"Then you shall see and become radiant, and your heart shall swell with joy." This certainly happens when the glory and the favor of the Lord is upon you.

"Because the abundance of the sea shall be turned to you, the wealth of the Gentiles shall come to you. The multitude of camels shall cover your land, the dromedaries of Midian and Ephah; all those from Sheba shall come; they shall bring gold and incense, and they shall proclaim the praises of the Lord."

You can reach a stage where the glory of the Lord comes so strongly upon your life that everyone will start to come and give you money. This is exciting, and I found that my ministry attracts people who give to me financially.

Some people read my books and are impressed with them. They are led by the Lord, by the Holy Spirit, to give to me. The Lord leads them to give me money.

I look forward to a day when I go out to the world, and I'm shining nearly every day. I have the gift of prophecy, and I can give total strangers a prophetic word. If they approach me all the time and want to talk to me, this would be a great way to share prophetic words.

This is one of my life verses. I actually discovered this verse after shining. I was reading my Bible once and came across this verse and said to myself, "This verse confirms who I am."

This promise in the Bible isn't just for me. This promise and prophecy can be true for your life also. Have you had days where people were staring at you? Do babies stare at you? Do people ask you for directions all the time? Do people open up to you? If these things are true, you are already manifesting a portion of this glory. I recommend that you read some books to find out more about the glory of the Lord.

Chapter 5

Isaiah 42:6–9

"I, the Lord, have called You in righteousness, and will hold Your hand; I will keep You and give You as a covenant to the people, as a light to the Gentiles, to open blind eyes, to bring out prisoners from the prison, those who sit in darkness from the prison house. I am the Lord, that is My name; and My glory I will not give to another, nor My praise to carved images. Behold, the former things have come to pass, and new things I declare; before they spring forth I tell you of them."

"I, the Lord, have called You in righteousness, and will hold Your hand." Many years ago, I read this verse. This passage meant a lot to me. This scripture is actually a prophecy over the life of Jesus Christ. That's why the word You is capitalized in that sentence. The hand refers to the hand of Jesus Christ. This is a promise from a father to a son. As God's Son, Jesus, read this in the synagogue, this was a personal letter from his father saying, "I, Your Father, am going to hold your hand and going to lead you in righteousness."

I was aware that it was a prophecy of Jesus's life, but when I read the scripture the first time, it was a *rhema* word, a living word for me. For many years before I collected other verses, this was my key life verse.

"I will keep You and give You as a covenant to the people, as a light to the Gentiles." This verse is saying, "I'll give you as a ransom." Jesus is a covenant to the people—the new covenant. His life and death became the new covenant. Jesus is saying to me through these verses if I take them on that he's going to give me to the people of God. He's going to give me to the Christian church. He's going to use my life and pour it out for the Christian church and as a light to the Gentiles. I'm not only going to be a prophet who ministers to the Christian church, but I'm also going to be an evangelist who shares a message from Jesus, a message of hope from Jesus with people that are non-Christians.

I've done that so far with my books, <u>Princess Diana Speaks from Heaven: A Divine Revelation</u> and <u>Michael Jackson Speaks from Heaven: A Divine Revelation</u>. Those two books are evangelistic. <u>The Parables of Jesus Made Simple: Updated and Expanded Edition</u> is also an evangelistic book.

I try and focus my life on not only ministering to Christians but on giving non-Christians an example of the love of Jesus too. Many times, when I go out to a shopping center or somewhere public, I approach total strangers and give them a personal prophecy, which is called prophetic evangelism. Jesus gave an example of this when he ministered to the Samaritan woman at the well with a prophetic word. I do this as well. Even though I might be called a prophet, I operate as an evangelist too. I feel that every Christian should be used as a light to both Christians and non-Christians.

Jesus was given as a light to direct Gentiles to himself. We know this because the whole village was attracted to his light. This verse promises me that I'm given as a covenant to the people of God. In Jewish times, a Gentile was anyone who was not a Jew. In today's terms, we can interpret the word Gentile as non-Christians. I shine my light to the Gentiles as well.

"To open blind eyes, to bring out prisoners from the prison, those who sit in darkness from the prison house." The phrase, "to open blind eyes," seems to refer to a healing ministry. Jesus would have and did heal the physically blind, but I personally think that this refers to people who are spiritually blind.

Jesus spoke about the blind guides and leading the blind and how both end up in the ditch. You can be in a Christian church and be blinded by religion, be blinded by what's taught. You might not receive fresh revelation.

A large percentage of Christians don't have the first idea about how to be led by the Spirit and how to have their lives directed by him each day. I practice so many fundamental things in my Christian life that the average Christian doesn't understand and doesn't walk in. So many Christians are blind to the truth, blind to the reality and the power of the gospel. This is a sad state of affairs.

I've been given as a covenant to the Christian church. I have laid down my life to educate the Christian church and to open their eyes so that they can see.

Jesus spoke in parables because he only wanted certain people to understand and to come to the knowledge of the truth. He hid the truth in his parables, and you really had to seek out the answer to the parable to find the truth.

This verse also means that you have to go to the darkness in order to reach someone in prison. You probably won't win a prostitute to the Lord unless you visit a brothel. You can't save a prisoner and bring the prisoner to the Lord unless you visit a prison. You can't heal someone who's sick unless you go to a hospital.

You actually have to go where the sinners are. You have to go to those who have issues. If you have a problem with sinners—

strippers, prostitutes, gays, homosexuals, drinkers, alcoholics, drug addicts, and gamblers— you won't go to the places they frequent, and you won't be a light to them. My life, however, has been a testimony of going to those places and being a light to those sorts of people.

For a year, I visited a brothel in Kings Cross in Sydney. I bought the prostitutes coffee and chocolates. I talked to them and laughed with them. They couldn't understand why I was doing these nice things for them. I told them, "Jesus cannot come here himself, so I'm coming here to bless you on his behalf."

"I am the Lord, that is My name; And My glory I will not give to another, nor My praise to carved images." The Lord wants to be the center of attention. He wants to be the one that's glorified. We spoke in the last chapter about the glory of the Lord coming upon me, but that's not to build up my own name or my own reputation. I'm not saying, "Hey! Look at me I'm shining. I'm so wonderful!" But the glory has to go to the Father, to the Lord Jesus to do all these things. Make sure your life points toward Jesus.

A friend of mine wrote about my books, saying that my books take you to various places with different scenery, but every sign in each scenic location points to Jesus. That was a very nice explanation of what my books do. They all point to Jesus.

"Behold, the former things have come to pass, and new things I declare; before they spring forth I tell you of them." The Lord is very aware of your life. If you seek out prophetic people, he can tell you about your future. He certainly knows your past and can use it to build your future. He has done this for me and is using everything I've been through to encourage readers as I share my experiences.

Do you feel that this passage that we have covered refers to you also? Do you feel that you have a calling on your life to affect the lives of non-Christians or Christians? Do you feel that you could be used to open the blind eyes of people? Do you think that you could be called to people that are sitting in darkness who have addictions and wayward lifestyles? This passage is a life verse for me, and perhaps it could be one for you, providing the necessary mission statement for your life.

Chapter 6

Matthew 5:14–16

"You are the light of the world. A city that is set on a hill cannot be hidden. Nor do they light a lamp and put it under a basket, but on a lampstand, and it gives light to all who are in the house. Let your light so shine before men, that they may see your good works and glorify your Father in heaven."

Jesus was the light in the last passage that we covered, a light to the Gentiles. Jesus also wants us to be a light. The Gospel of John tells us in chapter one that Jesus was the light of the world and he came to the earth and the people didn't recognize Him (paraphrased). Jesus wants us to be the light. He wants us to be full of the fruit of the Spirit: love, joy, peace, patience, goodness, faithfulness, kindness, gentleness, and self-control. (See Galatians 5:22–23.) He wants us to be the most understanding, compassionate, and kind people on the face of the planet. He doesn't want us to be people full of rules.

A non-Christian doesn't have to live by any rules other than the laws of society. They can be in sin, doing things that are dreadful, and we are still supposed to love them. We must still be example of Jesus. We're not to judge or condemn them. Many Christians want a non-Christian to transform and be without sin before they accept them, before they lead them to church and convince them to become a Christian. Non-Christians just don't like it. I have heard it said that you actually have to catch the fish first before you clean them. The church seems to want to do the opposite—clean up people before they're caught.

Jesus is saying, "You are the light of the world. A city that is set on the hill cannot be hidden." I had someone prophesy to me last week, saying that I was sitting on a hill, and my life was going forth throughout the world. They said that through all the people that are friends with me on Facebook and through the twelve hundred readers of my books each month, I am a city on a hill. I thought that was very encouraging because this verse is an integral part of my life.

The next verse says, "Nor do they light a lamp and put it under a basket, but on a lampstand, and it gives light to all who are in the house." When you enter a house, a church, or a building, your personal light should come into the building. You can carry the presence of the Lord in such a way that people might even manifest demons. If you walk close to them, they walk away from you. You need to be in a position where you carry love, acceptance, joy, peace, and kindness into the environment where you walk. You need to be able to bring Jesus and his love and kindness into any environment that you are in. This scripture is telling you not to put your Christianity under a basket when you go to work.

Don't hide the fact that you're a Christian. Instead put your Christian faith on the lampstand. But don't put your Christian faith on the lampstand by saying you despise sinners: prostitutes, gays, alcoholics, gamblers, the divorced. Don't bring all the negative aspects of Christianity into your workplace. Don't judge people or sinners, but be a light and be the person that you need to be.

Be there for your co-worker if her mother just died. Stay and work extra hours for your co-worker who's sick and feeling under the weather. Be there for that girl who is crying because she broke up with her boyfriend. She can't cope with the fact that this man that she loved has left her. Be there for the person who's being picked on at work, when others are being cruel to him or her. Be there for people who have a need. Be that tree with that good fruit that people can come and pick up and be sustained by.

The next verse is, "Let your light so shine before men, that they may see your good works and glorify your Father in heaven." This verse is saying to be a shining example so that people see your testimony and see the good works that you do. Let people see that you will stand up for others if bullying is happening. Let them see that you will have nothing to do with gossip.

When a shooter has rampaged through a school and killed multiple students, be the positive voice in that situation. You can bring light and demonstrate Jesus Christ and his personality. Don't be religious or hypocritical, full of judgment and condemnation of others. Be an example to others in your workplace and at church to follow. Set such a positive example that people want to become like you. Be so positive that people are amazed at how you carry yourself and how you talk and respond to different events and times of crisis in the nation. People are looking for answers; they're looking for a light, and they're looking for someone to follow.

I've meditated on this verse for so often and for so long that I've become this kind of person. I have to say that I don't have many issues with non-Christians. I normally have issues with people in the Christian church. They are the ones who come against me and speak out against me. Non-Christians seem to love me, and in that way, I'm a lot like Jesus. Jesus used to hang out with the sinners, and the religious people didn't like him.

You can find out more about how to be light in the world by reading my book, _Influencing Your World for Christ_.

Chapter 7

Daniel 12:3

"Those who are wise shall shine like the brightness of the firmament,
and those who turn many to righteousness like the stars forever and ever."

In a previous chapter, I mentioned Isaiah 60 and that the glory of the Lord would come upon you. You might think that that's just a random verse. But remember the last chapter and what Jesus said in Matthew 5:14–16. "You are the light of the world . . . . Let your light so shine before men, that they see your good works and glorify your father in heaven." Could Jesus be talking about the fact that you can literally shine physically so that others can see you?

Are you meant to be the light of the world and light up a whole household? Was Jesus literally saying that you would shine? It might be true. Isaiah 60 seems to back up the fact that people can truly shine. Some people think that the Bible is just talking figuratively here, not literally. I like to say that some scripture verses can speak figuratively and literally at the same time.

Daniel 12:3 says, "Those who are wise shall shine like the brightness of the firmament." Those who walk in the wisdom of God are essentially being led and directed by the Holy Spirit. They can shine like the brightness of the firmament or the stars above us. Daniel 12 refers to the end times and the last days. People in those days will "shine like the brightness of the firmament."

The next part says, "Those who turn many to righteousness like stars forever and ever." People who are walking in the wisdom of God are essentially walking in the ways of the Holy Spirit. They will shine like the stars above us. Those who lead many to Christ, those who direct people to live a righteous life, will shine like stars.

Many Christians are living religious and rule-based lives. They're sad with no purpose in their life. A large percentage of Christians have no idea why they're here and what their purpose is. But you can lead them and direct them to their purpose and encourage them and have them learn what Jesus taught. You can teach them to obey everything that Jesus taught and to walk like Jesus wanted them to walk. You will turn them to righteousness, which is right living.

Of course, if you lead a non-Christian to a Christian church and to faith, you've led them to righteousness too. Many people are led to the church, and yet they are led to religion and rule-based condemnation, guilt, and shame. The non-Christians actually end up worse off and feeling more discouraged about life than they did when they weren't saved. If you lead many people, including Gentiles, non-Christians, and Christians, to a perfect Spirit-led life, then you will shine like the stars forever and ever.

When I get to heaven, the glory on my skin will shine. I've heard testimonies of people in heaven, certain saints in heaven who shone with an amazing glory in heaven. Everyone knows who they are, which commands respect and honor in heaven. Not everyone in heaven looks the same. Different levels of glory are on each person's skin and body. You'll be respected and shine like a star forever and ever in heaven because of what you do on earth.

I choose to make my books as inexpensive as possible on Kindle so that the maximum number of people can read them. I'm making my talent work for me. I'm duplicating my resources to such a point that they are reaching the maximum number of people possible. My whole being is focused on eternal rewards.

I've written a book called *Living for Eternity: Life with Eternal Rewards in Mind*. That book tells you how to live your life so that you will receive maximum rewards in heaven for what you do. My whole life is focused on kingdom rewards. I'm focused on winning the hearts of as many people as possible into righteous living. That's my whole purpose, so I live for eternal rewards. I live to become one of the brightest shining people in heaven. Jesus talks about not storing your treasure on earth where moth and rust destroy, and thieves break in and steal, but he says to store your treasures in heaven where they will be safe and secure (Matthew 6:19–20).

I live a life so that I can store up maximum rewards in heaven. That's just the way I live. I don't live for fancy clothes, fast cars, or luxurious houses. I live so that my eternal reward is at its maximum, and that's just how I am. Anyone who has read all of my books or a large portion of my books will realize the sort of person that I am. I am fully intent on shining brightly in heaven. When you get to heaven and see me there, you'll recognize that I not only strove to shine like a star in heaven forever and ever, but I actually achieved it.

This passage of scripture seems to speak of a future event, and yet you will remember that Isaiah 60 was talking about life right now. Jesus was also talking about us shining our light. Jesus compelled us to do what he did and to love people like he did. It is entirely possible to stand out and shine in this life.

I like being around babies and seeing them stare at me. This tells me that my glory is shining all the time. Jesus does not want us to be passive. He wants us to be like him and to become lights in this world. Can you see yourself becoming one of these people that shine like stars?

Chapter 8

Jeremiah 1:5

"Before I formed you in the womb I knew you; before you were born I sanctified you; I ordained you a prophet to the nations."

Jeremiah 1:8-10

"'Do not be afraid of their faces, for I am with you to deliver you,' says the Lord. Then the Lord put forth His hand and touched my mouth, and the Lord said to me: 'Behold, I have put My words in your mouth. See, I have this day set you over the nations and over the kingdoms, to root out and to pull down, to destroy and to throw down, to build and to plant.'"

Here are more of my life verses. For me, a life verse personally applies and gives my life direction. The first passage is, "Before I formed you in the womb I knew you; before you were born I sanctified you; I ordained you a prophet to the nations." In the last twenty years, I found out that I was called to be a prophet. I read this verse once again as I was reading through the Bible, and it jumped out at me. It was amazing!

When I was born, the umbilical cord was wrapped around my neck. I was catatonic blue; I almost died from suffocation. I was called a blue baby, a baby that was seriously lacking oxygen. I was taken from the womb straight to an oxygen machine to make sure that I lived. The medical professionals panicked a little when I was born.

Satan knew of my birth and knew that I was a prophet. Just like Jesus and Moses, he tried to put a stop to my life. Before I was born, Jesus decided that I was going to live to be a prophet. I have heard a prophet speak on this subject, and he says that many prophets have difficult births.

I consistently have at least twelve hundred books going out to the nations every month. I'm already a prophet to the nations. I could travel to six churches every month and preach to two hundred people at each church. I'm preaching to that many people per month through my books. I have eight hundred and fifty articles on the internet that reach a lot of people. I also have over a thousand YouTube videos, and many people watch them each month. So before being invited to speak at churches, I am impacting people. In the years to come, when God is ready, I will start to travel to the nations of the world.

Isaiah 60 also says that, "Kings will come to the glory of your rising." I know that in the future, I'm going to consult kings and leaders of countries. That's been prophesied over me many times. This is a key verse for me and one that I stand on.

"'Do not be afraid of their faces, for I am with you to deliver you,' says the Lord." I continue to write controversial books with interviews of saints from heaven. This is God speaking to me. "Do not be afraid of their faces." The Lord is saying that I shouldn't be afraid of what people will say. I shouldn't be afraid of people calling me a warlock, which some people do, or a false prophet, which many people do. The Lord says, "I'm with you to deliver you." That's really encouraging to me.

The next sentence is, "The Lord put forth His hand and touched my mouth, and the Lord said to me." That's really touching to me because that's what happened to Isaiah. A coal was put on his mouth to cleanse him. I am really touched that the Lord has done that to me.

The next verse is, "Behold, I have put My words in your mouth. See, I have this day set you over the nations and over the kingdoms, to root out and to pull down, to destroy and to throw down, to build and to plant."

Many people who feel they're called to be prophets or called as a spokesman for God will mistakenly pull down ministries and attack ministers. They quote all these teachings that the people say and the things that people preach, and they pull down ministers and accuse others of being a false prophet or a false teacher. They say that anyone who follows these ministries is deceived. It's fine to pull down wrong doctrine and wrong teaching, but you have to replace it, to build and to plant. Many people come against false teaching, but they don't replace it with the truth. These heresy hunters need a little balance in their lives.

In the future, when I'm ministering and coming against a certain teaching, I'm going to spend the second half of the sermon preaching the truth. I might come into a church and discern that they're being led astray by the prosperity doctrine. I might start to preach against the prosperity doctrine and say what's wrong with it. Then, I'll teach about what prosperity in the Lord looks like and the proper way to give to the Lord. I'll talk about the proper attitude to have toward the Lord and kingdom finances. The job of the prophet is to not only pull down wrong structures but to build up and rebuild. If you can, just do the rebuilding, which will make people question the false beliefs they have.

If you preach the truth and the correct ideas, the new revelation can overtake people, and they can come out of the error that they're in. You don't have to spend the majority of your message and your time pulling down ministries, teachers, and ministers of the gospel. The majority of your time should be spent proclaiming truth and encouraging and building up people. You've probably seen people coming against ministries and pulling down people and calling others false prophets on Facebook.

Billy Graham died as I was preparing this book. A lot of people were attacking him on social media, saying he's a false teacher and a false Christian. Anyone that respects him is also judged by these people. I didn't have one person in my Facebook feed speak negatively against him during the week after he died. But friends of mine have been upset with some of the things others have posted. Anyone can expose error, but that is only half of the job. You are also called to replace the error with the truth and rebuild the people who were exposed to it.

I'm called as a prophet, and I have a purpose to go to the nations. I also have a calling to come against false teaching and error and replace it with the good news of the gospel and the true news of the kingdom of God.

Do you have a call to impact the nations? Are these verses applicable to you also? You could affect the nations simply by writing a popular blog or posting to a YouTube channel. Perhaps you could write books like I do. Are you called to tear down false teachings and false structures and rebuild and replant? Though this chapter might not have been applicable to all of my readers, it could apply to more of you than you know.

Chapter 9

John 6:8–9

"One of His disciples, Andrew, Simon Peter's brother, said to Him, "There is a lad here who has five barley loaves and two small fish, but what are they among so many?"

This is a strategic scripture to get your hands on and powerful in my life. About fifteen years ago, I was doing evangelism in the streets of Sydney. I had a bullhorn, and I'd sing certain songs and then preach a sermon about what the songs were saying. Sometimes I would just sit down with my Bible with the bullhorn and read from the Bible and teach just like I'm doing here.

I was witnessing a lot and spending my days doing that. I was on a disability pension, so I had money supplied to me to live each week. I was living very cheaply. I received this prophecy from a person who was practicing their gift on me.

"I see the picture of the boy with two fish and five barley loaves. The fact that he had barley loaves and that they weren't made out of wheat meant that he was a poor boy because barley cost less than wheat. I got an image of that little boy. God tells me that the little boy is you. You don't have much. You don't have a lot of resources, but everything that you do have, you're giving to the Lord. You're giving in service to the Lord. The Lord just wants to encourage you and say that he understands that you're poor. He understands that you haven't got much to give, but he's happy with you for giving him your whole life and everything that you have."

I read that prophecy when I was on a break. I received it in an email and printed it out. I was having a coffee with my bullhorn beside me. I read that, and I cried. It just meant so much to me.

From that day on, this life verse has become so important to me. I use it from time to time when I give a prophetic word for someone that has requested a prophetic word from my ministry. I tell them that they're a little boy with two fish and five loaves.

I really don't have much, but I've given everything to the Lord, and now I minister to people. I wasn't born with a lot. I don't have a great education in school. I was picked on, and I was lonely. I was misunderstood and strange. I was a sad little boy because I was struggling emotionally and spiritually. I had a hard time concentrating at school and did not get good grades. I didn't do well in school. My favorite subject was English, but I failed it. But now I'm happy because this is my forty-second book.

I had an English teacher that gave me a grade of ten out of ten once on a paper. It had no red grammar and spelling mistakes markings on it, which was unusual for me. I questioned him, and he said, "See me after class." After class, he said, "You can't ever get more than eight out of ten, Matthew, because your grammar and spelling are atrocious. You have so many mistakes that the maximum mark that I can give you is eight. But you have a lot of eights, don't you?"

I said, "Yes, I do."

He said, "That's because you're one of the best writers that I have come across in my life. Anyone can do well at grammar and spelling, but not many people can write stories like you write. You're a fabulous writer. You go on and become a writer. Hire an editor who can correct your spelling. I'm just a simple teacher, and I'm not that smart. I can correct your grammar and spelling, but I can't write as well as you can." That conversation was a highlight of my life. Since then, I've written forty-two books.

I've never had much to bring to the table. I wasn't highly educated; I didn't go to a university. I never went to Bible college. I really don't have a lot of money. I suffered half of my life with a mental illness. As a prophet, I've been rejected and misunderstood by many people. I'm not loved by too many people, and I've had very few friends in my life. I just don't have a lot to offer. I'm very much like this little boy who gave his lunch to Jesus, not knowing that he would do a miracle with it. I would have given Jesus my lunch also if I were given the opportunity and if I were there on that day. I would have offered Jesus food because I have a gift of giving, and I love to give.

I really identify with this little boy. That's what makes my life so precious because I know I don't have a lot to offer, but I do the very best I can. Some people who are reading this book and who've read twenty or thirty of my books will think to themselves, "Is he kidding? He's amazing. He comes out with such incredible things. He's my favorite author. What's he saying about himself?"

That's what makes this so special. Jesus has taken my life and made it special. He's taken my failure in English. He's taken my desire to write. He's taken what that teacher of mine said. He's allowed me to start a ministry that earns me money, and he's used that money. He's used my ability to write and made it into something special. He's duplicated my gift and then made it into a miracle.

Who would think that someone on a disability pension could reach twelve hundred people a month? Who would think that someone who's never attended Bible college could have so many people bringing him testimonies of radically changed lives? Who am I? I'm just a simple person, which is why this passage or scripture is one of my life verses. Whenever I identify myself with this little boy, Jesus can do multiplication miracles with my life.

Are you a simple person who has given Jesus everything? Do you relate to this little boy? Can you see yourself giving Jesus your five loaves and two fish and witnessing Jesus do a miracle with your offering? Perhaps right up till now, this was just a story in the Bible, and you never took it personally. What does the story look like now? Can you say that you have given Jesus your all? Are you also like a little child who simply wants to bless the Lord with your gift?

Chapter 10

John 14:21

"He who has My commandments and keeps them, it is he who loves Me. And he who loves Me will be loved by My Father, and I will love him and manifest Myself to him."

In the year 2000, I was walking down the street, and I came across some people giving out a free book. When they gave me the book, they asked for a donation. I didn't mind that; they were Christians. I started talking to them about the books, and they had tracts, so I took a couple. They were called "The Jesus Christians." I asked them why they called themselves that. They said, "Well, we want to identify ourselves as Christians that obey Jesus. A lot of Christians follow rules and teachings of the church and religion, but they don't obey Jesus. We prefer to live like Jesus taught." This really fascinated me.

One of the tracts was called the top forty. I read the tract that listed forty commands of Jesus, forty things that Jesus told his followers to do. It was fascinating. I took the tract to my mother, and I said, "Can you open the Gospels and look up these forty commands? Find the scripture references in all the Gospels where these commands are spoken. If you find any more commands, add them to the forty."

She went through the Bible for a month or so and ended up with fifty commands, the fifty commands of Jesus. Many people don't know that these exist. I would say that very few Christians in the church know that Jesus has fifty commandments.

John 14:21 says, "He who has My commandments and keeps them, it is he who loves Me." Who loves Jesus? Someone who says they love him, or someone who knows his fifty commands and keeps them? Jesus identifies those that love him as those who know and keep the fifty commands of Jesus. It's that simple. Later on, John says, "He that loves me obeys my commands, and he who does not obey my commands does not love me" (John 14:23–24 paraphrased).

You can read who loves Jesus. Is it the person at church with their hands in the air, singing songs to Jesus, "Oh, I love you?" Or is it the person who not only sings worship songs to Jesus but who actually knows and obeys his commands? It's very easy to become legalistic about these and say, "You have to obey Jesus's commands, or you don't really love him." I don't want to give the impression that I'm saying that you have to follow a whole bunch of rules.

Many great teachers would say I am doing that. But obeying Jesus's commands brings benefits, and "He who loves me will be loved by my Father and I will love him and I will manifest myself to him." What happens there? He that obeys the commands and shows that he loves Jesus will be loved by Jesus, will be loved by the Father, and Jesus will manifest himself to him. What's going on there? Do Jesus and the Father love certain people more than they love other people? If you love Jesus and you find out what his commands are and you start to practice and obey them, is he saying that he will love you more than he loves people who don't obey his commands? That might be hard for people to understand.

There are levels of achievement. People might be good at math, but certain people can excel at math while others can be geniuses. You might be at a starting level as a Christian. You can be at an intermediate level as a Christian, and you can be at an exceptional level as a Christian. Everything has levels.

It seems that Jesus loves people when they're walking and doing everything he teaches. You can imagine a teacher, an English teacher, being really interested in his student that not only reads assigned texts and does all his homework, but he reads the suggested texts, the suggested books, that the teacher recommends and can have discussions with his teacher about those extra books. Of course, the relationship with that student who's doing everything that he's required to do and more is a closer relationship.

One of the promises also is that Jesus will manifest himself to you. What does that mean? When you start to obey Jesus, one of the meanings of this is that you start to develop his character. You start to come to know the mind of Christ. You start to understand how Christ operates. You start to form an impression of who Jesus really is because you're living your life the way that he told you to live it.

Jesus said in Matthew that "he who hears his commands and obeys him is like a wise man who's built his house upon a rock and when the winds and rain come, the house stood. But the person who listens to what he says and doesn't obey him is like the foolish man who built his house upon the sand." (See Matthew 7:24–27, paraphrased.)

Jesus is saying, "Hey, I said all of these things in the Gospels. You've heard me say them, but you're not doing them. You're foolish." I hope that this is not condemning you. I hope that you have a sense of conviction here to find out what the fifty commands are and to start to obey them. You can find the link to them here: "Fifty Commands of Jesus." If you are reading the paperback, you can search "The Fifty Commands of Jesus" on Google and find my ezine article on the subject.

One way Jesus will manifest himself to you is by showing you his character and his personality as you obey him. The second way you can interpret what it means for him to manifest himself to you is that he'll show up. Jesus will start to appear to you in visions and walk and talk with you. You can be invited to heaven, and you'll be able to see Jesus there and meet him on earth. You can walk and talk with Jesus and become like him. He'll manifest himself and his personality in your life. This is one of my key life verses, and I live out this verse.

I don't perfectly obey all his commands because I'm still learning, but I do the best that I can as I live my life. I understand what his commands are, and they're the focal point of my life. I have a friend who is writing a book about the commands of Jesus that will be out in the next year. That will be a really interesting book for you to read.

This is one of my key life verses, and I often mention it in my books. I thought I'd give you a little understanding about why it's one of my life verses.

You need to know that the more you know about your faith, the better you can live it out. Living the commands of Jesus allows you to live like the first disciples did. This means that you are living your life on the rock, and as life becomes difficult in years to come, you will be fine no matter what happens, no matter what storms may come. The last thing I want to do is give you more religious rules to follow. I see the commands as keys to life, secret keys since many Christians have no idea that they exist. I personally believe that this verse is the key to my supernatural lifestyle.

Chapter 11

Luke 7:36–50

"Then one of the Pharisees asked Him to eat with him. And He went to the Pharisee's house, and sat down to eat. And behold, a woman in the city who was a sinner, when she knew that Jesus sat at the table in the Pharisee's house, brought an alabaster flask of fragrant oil, and stood at His feet behind Him weeping; and she began to wash His feet with her tears, and wiped them with the hair of her head; and she kissed His feet and anointed them with the fragrant oil. Now when the Pharisee who had invited Him saw this, he spoke to himself, saying, 'This Man, if He were a prophet, would know who and what manner of woman this *is* who is touching Him, for she is a sinner.'"

"And Jesus answered and said to him, 'Simon, I have something to say to you.'

"So he said, 'Teacher, say it.'

"'There was a certain creditor who had two debtors. One owed five hundred denarii, and the other fifty. And when they had nothing with which to repay, he freely forgave them both. Tell Me, therefore, which of them will love him more?'

"Simon answered and said, 'I suppose the one whom he forgave more.'

"And He said to him, 'You have rightly judged.' Then He turned to the woman and said to Simon, 'Do you see this woman? I entered your house; you gave Me no water for My feet, but she has washed My feet with her tears and wiped them with the hair of her head. You gave Me no kiss, but this woman has not ceased to kiss My feet since the time I came in. You did not anoint My head with oil, but this woman has anointed My feet with fragrant oil. Therefore I say to you, her sins, which are many, are forgiven, for she loved much. But to whom little is forgiven, the same loves little.'

"Then He said to her, 'Your sins are forgiven.'

"And those who sat at the table with Him began to say to themselves, 'Who is this who even forgives sins?'

"Then He said to the woman, 'Your faith has saved you. Go in peace.'"

In this passage of scripture, one of the Pharisees invited Jesus to speak with him. Halfway through the meal, a woman burst into the gathering and wept on Jesus's feet. She then untied her hair and wiped his feet with her hair. She plastered his feet with alabaster, a very expensive oil that released a beautiful scent into the whole house.

The Pharisee spoke to himself that if this Jesus was a prophet, he would know what sort of woman was touching him. He essentially called the woman unclean and judged Jesus for allowing himself to be touched by a prostitute.

Jesus answered him with a story of two men in debt. One was forgiven a debt of five hundred denarii while the other was forgiven a debt of fifty denarii. Jesus asked which man would love him more.

Someone answered that the man who was forgiven more would love more.

Jesus agreed and then honored the woman for her gracious behavior. He observed that on the other hand, Simon had not washed his feet or greeted him with a kiss or anointed him with oil. (These were all traditional customs of the day.)

Jesus then said, "Therefore, I say to you, her sins, which are many, are forgiven, for she loved much. But to whom little is forgiven, the same loves little" (v. 47).

I really relate to this story. Early in my life, I acted on homosexual urges. But when I moved to Sydney, I went to King's Cross and slept with a prostitute. I then became addicted to the services of prostitutes, which went on for many years. That addiction was a real struggle for me. So I related to a prostitute touching Jesus's feet.

But this life verse applies to me because of Jesus's statement here. "Therefore, I say to you, her sins, which are many, are forgiven, for she loved much. But to whom little is forgiven, the same loves little."

I spent my whole life sinning. I've sinned so many times. I slept with prostitutes hundreds and hundreds of times. I sin so much. You know, anyone who has read many of my books knows that about me. If you haven't read my other books and if this is the first book of mine that you've read, you might not know that, which might turn you off to me and my ministry. But this is my life verse because I'm like that woman.

I love Jesus so much because I've sinned so much and done so many things that are wrong. I've abused hundreds of women sexually by hiring them to sleep with me. I've been such a dreadful sinner, and yet the more you are forgiven, the more you'll love Jesus. It's amazing that when a person sins, it actually puts a gap between you and Jesus until you confess your sins and come back to Jesus. He then closes that gap and restores you.

Satan loves to beat you up and condemn you when you sin. Committing sins against Jesus can really damage your relationship with him, and I wouldn't recommend that anyone live this type of lifestyle, one that I've lived for many years.

But I wouldn't like to be the person who's only sinned a little bit and who only loves Jesus a little bit. I want a thirsty and hungry and passionate love for Jesus. I pursue Jesus with everything that I have. I enjoy all of the following:
- Jesus
- his scriptures
- worship music
- books about Jesus
- talking to people about Jesus
- sharing Jesus
- teaching about the righteous life
- teaching people how to grow close to Jesus
- talking to angels
- talking to saints from heaven
- talking to Jesus
- having visions of him and
- being led by the Spirit every day.

My relationship with Jesus is so close. We're so tight. In the last chapter, we talked about how Jesus and his Father love you when you obey Jesus's commands. Jesus and the Father really love me. The more that they loved me, the more they shared their friends with me. They share the angels with me.

I meet angels all the time. They share their lives and their hearts with me and so do the Father and Jesus. They are so in love with me, and I'm so in love with them. This is because I've been such a wretched sinner in my life and have sinned so much. I've been forgiven for so much that I have an extraordinary love and passion for Jesus.

This might not help people who've lived a righteous and obedient life. But it gives insight into who I am and how I became so passionate and so close to Jesus so that I can go to heaven whenever I like. I can talk to saints from the Bible anytime I like. I can meet any angels that I choose to meet. I have an all-access pass to the kingdom of heaven. How do you reach a point like that? You reach that point when Jesus loves you and when he adores you, and you have this amazing relationship with him.

This is one of my life verses, and it would have been harder to explain this verse if I didn't talk about the homosexuality and the prostitute addiction. I hope that didn't turn you off, but I encourage you to press in and pursue Jesus with everything that you have.

This passage in the Bible has given me many hours of comfort. The Holy Spirit knew what we needed in the Bible to encourage us. Have you lived a life with a lot of mistakes and sinful behavior? This passage is for you. If you have been forgiven much, then it is only natural for you to love much. I hope this passage has encouraged you.

Chapter 12

Romans 8:28

"And we know that all things work together for good to those who love God, to those who are the called according to His purpose."

This verse of scripture has carried me for more than thirty years. I have been meditating on some scriptures for five, ten, twenty years. But I've been standing on this scripture for thirty or forty years.

This scripture means everything, *everything* to me. All of the sin that I've committed: homosexuality, bisexuality, sleeping with prostitutes, sleeping with women outside of marriage, jealousy, envy, gossiping, bad relationships, a failed marriage, losing my son, not talking to my son, seeing my son only once in eighteen years, my mental illness, and all the other sins I've committed. It includes all the good times, all the bad times, every Bible verse I've read, and everything that's ever happened in my life. All these things work together for good because I love God and I'm called according to his good purpose.

It doesn't matter what I've done although I'm not excusing sin. I'm not saying to go out and sin and live a reckless life. I certainly endeavor to live a holy and righteous life now. Everything I've done, everything I've experienced, and everything I've gone through—even my recent heart troubles and almost dying—all of those things will work together for good because I love God and because I'm called according to his purpose.

If you really understood this verse and got a hold of it, if you could meditate on this verse for many years of your life, if you could understand this verse and let it burn deep into your spirit, you would do well. You can let a verse go deep into your spirit when you quote it and recite it and claim it for yourself for years. That's how it becomes living within you. It becomes a testimony in you.

I don't lose many readers by telling them about my sin. I don't lose many people by talking about my shortfalls. Instead, I win the hearts of people who say, "Well, he's really honest and transparent. It's so amazing how he can come out with all those sins that would normally be hidden in the past and hidden by people in ministry. Why is he sharing about those sins? He must want us to know the truth. He must want to share his whole heart with us and not hide anything or hold anything back. This makes him seem like a real person and not just someone who doesn't know what it's like to struggle in life."

I have no problem confessing my sins, my shortfalls, and my failures before you because I know I'm forgiven. I know I'm loved. You know, Jesus is sitting on my couch right now smiling at me as I'm working on this book. Jesus is real to me. My life is a testimony. I failed English with a grade of 41 percent. But I have successfully written forty-two books that people love.

Some people have thirty-five of my books on their Kindle. I don't know many authors who have written more than forty books. Stephen King has written many books, and another friend and the owner of the publishing company that I use has written about sixty books. Joyce Myer has released more than a hundred books. Even so, forty-two books from someone who failed English and who the world would call hopeless as a writer is amazing.

I might be a hopeless writer. I've improved as I have been writing, but I have a tremendous editor. She works magic on my books. And my proofreader works magic as well. We produce great books, starting with my raw content. My editor then rewrites and edits as needed. Then the book is proofread, and it comes out perfectly. This all starts from a good story.

You can live your life and be sure that God can turn around anything in your life: any hurtful thing, any bad thing, any disease, any trouble, any heartache, any doubt, any struggle, or anything that comes against you.

We all love a movie where the underdog succeeds. We all like to hear about a struggling baseball team that goes on to the majors and wins the playoffs and becomes the world champions. We all like the story of the girl that everyone rejected who went on to become a movie star. We all like stories of people with no hope who persevered and endured. They had patience and overcame difficult circumstances, becoming winners.

We love stories about President Trump and others like him. Your president in the United States was just a simple man, following his father, who was a builder. He wasn't born with a silver spoon in his mouth. He has since made something of his life. Now he's leading a country.

God knows your struggles, your trials, and what you've been through. But if you trust in the promise of this verse, God can use your life to glorify himself. He can use all your hardships, trials, struggles, and hard times and can turn them around and bring glory to his name.

I was sexually abused. My father was an angry man. I had few friends. I've been lonely all my life. I've been rejected and misunderstood. I've wanted to kill myself three or four times. I've had a mental illness for twenty years. All these things have come against me to stop me, to hold me back, to keep me from moving toward the destiny that God had for me.

Twenty years ago, I counted my near-death experiences and found that there'd been thirteen attempts on my life. I'm here to say that all things worked together for good. No matter what has happened to you, you can glorify God. I hope that you're encouraged and that you learned some things about me in this chapter.

God has an agenda for everyone that lives as does Satan. In no way was Satan going to allow me to become a success. I am currently working with a counselor to remove some strongholds in my life that have been preventing me from doing all that God has called me to do. I was told by God that I would need more healing, and I pray that I have the courage to stick it out and be healed of all my pain. The verses in the Bible can be powerful and work wonders in our lives if we put them into practice and stand on them.

Chapter 13

Ephesians 3:20

"Now to him who is able to do exceedingly abundantly above all that we ask or think, according to the power that works in us."

What a wonderful verse! I came across this verse about six years ago, and it powerfully impacted me. I don't know if I came across the verse in a book or as I was simply reading the Bible. I've read most of the verses that I've mentioned in this book in the Bible, and the Holy Spirit illuminated them to me.

I'm really pleased today that the Holy Spirit illuminated this verse to me. I want to explain this verse and what it means to me and what it might mean to you in this chapter. I hope that you're really encouraged by what I say.

"Now to him who is able to do exceedingly abundantly above all that we ask or think." This verse means that God can do exceedingly and abundantly more than we can think about, than we can dream about, and than we can pray about. So whatever we ask for in prayer, whatever we dream about, whatever we think about, God can do way above and beyond that—abundantly and exceedingly more.

How many of you are living that life? How many of you are living a life where God has done exceedingly and abundantly more than you ever thought about? Can you testify to that being true in your life? Can you get a hold of that scripture and meditate on it for a few years so that it manifests in your life? Can you bring that passage to manifestation in your life? How would you like to have God do exceedingly and abundantly more than your dreams?

Imagine receiving the answers to your dreams. I would say that this is true for Donald Trump. He is one of my favorite people. I would say that he is doing exceedingly abundantly more than he could ever ask or think. I think he dreamed of becoming the President. He has certainly been talking about it for twenty years. But I reckon that he is so proud of himself. He is the most powerful man in the world. He has achieved exceedingly and abundantly more than he ever thought. What will he do after being President of the United States? Everything after that sounds like a demotion. I hope that he serves for eight years and then becomes a consultant to the other presidents that follow him.

I mentioned before that my school teacher said that I should become a writer. I did exactly that. I wrote a book on prostitutes, which I worked on and edited for about ten years. I edited it for so long that I just needed a proofreader to go through it, and then I was going to self-publish it.

But Jesus told me to throw out the book. The Holy Spirit highlighted a verse in the Bible to me. I felt the verse was saying that I needed to throw out my book. So I asked Jesus, "Is the Holy Spirit telling me to throw out my book?"

He said, "Yes. In fact, you're not going to enjoy church tonight unless you throw away the book."

I had held onto the book for many years, believing that it would launch my career in ministry. I dreamed of it for ten years. My whole hope was built on that book. I pulled out the printed manuscript and then threw that out. I found the disc that it was recorded on and threw it away. I went to the hard drive of my computer and deleted the Word file. I completely got rid of that book. I threw out my dream. Then, years later, Jesus led me to write again.

Now, as you read this book, it's my forty-second book. I have launched my career through books, and people all over the world are being affected by my books. Many people tell me that my books have totally transformed their lives. I just see myself as the little boy with loaves and fishes. I simply see myself as the chief of sinners, like Paul used to say about himself. (See 1 Timothy 1:5.)

I don't see myself as anyone special or amazing. But God has done exceedingly and abundantly above my dreams. I'm happy that I have friends on Facebook and that I can minister to them. I'm happy that people write to me and that my books are changing lives. I look forward to a time when I'm going to be traveling the world, ministering, speaking at conferences, and becoming everything that God created me to be. I look forward to God eclipsing my dreams and Jesus doing exceedingly and abundantly more than I could ask or think.

I look forward to everything I dream of coming to pass. I look forward to traveling the world, teaching people how to hear from Jesus, and leading prophetic schools.

I look forward to learning how to heal and becoming an experienced healer. I look forward to tens of thousands of people coming to conferences that I teach. I look forward to the exceedingly and the abundantly more than I can think or imagine. I can think up some amazing things.

I can think of big things. If Jesus can think bigger, if Jesus can do bigger, that will be wonderful. Even though I failed English, I'm achieving more than most people have achieved in their lifetime. I have just begun to start. I haven't really even made it far in my journey. You know, the fact that I have written forty-two books is great, but I look forward to writing a hundred books and to thousands of people reading my books.

I look forward to even becoming a New York Times bestselling author one day. Wouldn't that be great? That would be exceedingly, abundantly more than I could think. Well, now I thought it, so maybe I will write more than one best seller.

I encourage you to ponder this verse and think of the things that you have been dreaming of and imagine the Lord, through the power of the Holy Spirit, achieving abundantly more than you could ask for.

This verse is not just a verse for the lucky few but a verse for you to ponder on, to claim, and to live out. The Holy Spirit can do amazing things in our lives if we just allow him to work with us and through us.

Chapter 14

Now, we're going to switch gears and get into some harder teaching. Even so, I am still talking about my life verses. So I need to make these points about what these verses mean.

1 John 2:15–17 (NLT)

"Do not love this world nor the things it offers you, for when you love the world, you do not have the love of the Father in you. For the world offers only a craving for physical pleasure, a craving for everything we see, and pride in our achievements and possessions. These are not from the Father, but are from this world. And this world is fading away, along with everything that people crave. But anyone who does what pleases God will live forever."

The end of the passage says anyone who does what pleases God will live forever. Earlier, I mentioned that those who know and obey the commandments of Jesus show that they love Jesus. God loves them and is happy with them. What makes Jesus happy and what pleases God and bring us to eternal life is obedience to Jesus.

I want to emphasize that first point. "Do not love the world nor the things it offers you, for when you love the world, you do not have the love of the Father in you." How do you do that? How do you live in this world without loving the things of the world? How do you remain unattached to the things of the world?

Do you focus on ministry? Do you focus on what pleases God? Do you spend your money on what builds the kingdom and what prospers his kingdom? Or do you focus on buying what makes you happy?

The world only offers a craving for physical pleasure. Every advertisement is trying to sell you the same thing whether or not you know it. You buy brands and advertised products. Otherwise, you wouldn't know them. Not many people walk through a shopping center and buy brands that they've never seen advertised.

How many times do you walk through a shopping center and pick clothes, sunglasses, or candles that weren't first advertised to you? We live for physical pleasure. The whole capitalistic world, our democratic society, depends on us buying things. The whole financial world functions as it does because people buy things.

John was saying not to live that way, not to crave everything we see. You might see a Porsche or a nice four-wheel drive and want it for yourself. You see your neighbor has it, or someone you know has a new Rav4 or a new Mercedes, and you suddenly desire it. You might crave everything you see. John says don't live like that. When we want what others have, we are coveting.

We take pride in our achievements and possessions. How many people buy things because their friends bought them first or to impress their friends? How many people buy possessions to show them off?

When people walk into a home, they say to the homeowner, "This is a beautiful home. You've decorated it so well." That is pride in achievements and possessions. We live to impress others. The whole world of fashion is dressing up to impress others. But poor people in Africa can dress well and be fashionable, looking very nice. Poor people in India have beautiful saris.

Who are we trying to impress? Even the poor can dress up nicely. Jesus said in Matthew 6:28 that even the lilies of the fields dress themselves better than King Solomon was arrayed.

How do you live so that you're not interested in those things? How do you live without focusing on those things? You have to have other priorities.

I have a friend, Praying Medic, an author who is entirely focused on serving God. He has a nice house and a beautiful wife and grown children. He's a successful author. He totally focuses on reporting politics to Christians as a source of true and reliable news. God has changed his agenda from writing Christian books into a political commentator.

He's not being paid for that by an employer. People don't send him money because he's a commentator. He does it for the Lord. He lives fairly well, but he lives by faith. I'm so proud of him.

I'm so proud of myself and how I live. From time to time, I watch TV when I'm not busy doing other things, but I don't live a life of extravagance. I think the key to living a life not focused on the things of the world is knowing and living out your life's purpose.

Of course, money and possessions aren't terrible. These things won't send you to hell. But your focus should forever be on God's kingdom. If you don't have the skill set to actually heal people or prophesy to people or witness to people, you need to find resources to teach you those things and practice them because Jesus wants his people to expand his kingdom.

If you don't know how to expand the kingdom or where to give, you can send $210 to Iris Ministries at this link here. You can support and pay for training a pastor from one of the bush towns in

Mozambique. You can pay for five years of Bible college for him and his accommodations while he's training for three months a year. You can train and support a pastor to preach the kingdom for the rest of his life. God will credit everyone that he saves and everyone that he brings into the kingdom to your eternal account. You could spend your money by supporting one of these pastors instead of spending money to satisfy your greed.

My whole life is devoted to God and to others. I don't know any other way to live. I don't follow the world's trends or seek after the things of the world. I live this way because this is how God has taught me to live. He showed me this passage many years ago, and he has taught me to focus on his kingdom. I pray that you also learn to live out this verse and learn to serve God with your whole life.

Chapter 15

James 4:2–4

"You lust and do not have. You murder and covet and cannot obtain. You fight and war. Yet, you do not have because you do not ask. You ask and do not receive, because you ask amiss, that you may spend it on your pleasures.

"Adulterers and adulteresses! Do you not know that friendship with this world is enmity with God? Whoever therefore wants to be a friend of this world makes himself an enemy of God."

This passage also has a serious tone. If you've read a lot of my books, I often quote this verse. Many countries go to war because of resources. If you believe in some right-wing teachings, some of the wars overseas have been more about oil, control, and resources than for the actual reasons that they say on the news.

"You lust and you do not have. You murder and covet and cannot obtain. You fight and war. Yet, you do not have because you do not ask."

America used to go to war over oil. Now, President Trump is opening up the oil reserves in America, and America will produce its own oil. Perhaps they won't have as many wars.

Some years ago, the Holy Spirit showed me the verse about not having if you don't ask. He told me, "You never ask us for anything, Matthew. You need to ask us for things that will improve your life." I believed that the Lord gave me my daily bread and supplied every need I had. I had believed Philippians 4:19: "He shall supply all your need according to His riches in glory." I used to just rely on that understanding, and I didn't ask Jesus for anything extra.

I had conversations with Jesus, but I didn't really ask for things. Last year, the Holy Spirit and Jesus told me to ask for money to finance my next book. I had faith to ask for five hundred dollars, so I asked for that. The next day, someone donated that exact amount.

I again asked for five hundred dollars. This time, someone donated seven hundred dollars. I again asked for five hundred dollars, and someone donated twelve hundred dollars. So I asked for a thousand dollars, and someone donated seventeen hundred dollars. I needed all that money because I had to edit a book of more than a hundred thousand words, which cost six thousand, five hundred dollars. The book was *The Parables of Jesus Made Simple: Updated and Expanded Edition*.

Now when I have a need, I have learned to ask. But the reason that many people ask and they do not have it supplied is because they are asking amiss to spend it on their own pleasures.

One of the main reasons that people can't get kingdom finances for themselves is because they want them for their selfish pleasures: a bigger car, a fancier TV, or a more expensive house. They are asking for their own pleasures. They're not asking for things for the kingdom or to sow back into the kingdom. People need to align themselves with the kingdom of God.

Why are you here? You need to know your purpose. You need to know why you're here. I wrote a book called *Finding Your Purpose in Christ*. If you are struggling with understanding your purpose, that would be a great book for you to read. When you know why you're here, you can live out your life accordingly.

"Adulterers and adulteresses, do you not know that friendship with this world is enmity with God? Whoever therefore wants to be a friend of this world makes himself an enemy of God."

When James says adulterers and adulteresses, he's talking about committing spiritual adultery against Jesus when you lust for the things of the world and spend your money on possessions.

You're treating those possessions as more important to you than Jesus. Of course, Jesus doesn't want you to be homeless, and he wants you to have appropriate accommodations. He wants you to be able to drive your kids to school and get to work. But you don't need to be excessive. You can choose the simple things. You don't have to have the eighty thousand dollar car but can buy the ten thousand dollar car.

You don't have to buy the half million dollar house but can buy the hundred thousand dollar house. You don't have to have the best of everything until you earn an income that allows you to afford those things. James says that when you're a friend of the world and acting like the world, you are an enemy of God.

Why am I God's friend? Because all my resources go to the kingdom. I very rarely buy clothes or things for myself because I prefer to invest in eternal rewards.

I'm starting to minister in churches now. I will have to buy some nice clothes so that I can dress appropriately when I preach. I'm frugal, not cheap. All my money goes toward the kingdom, and I spend two thousand dollars a month producing books that I sell for ninety-nine cents on Kindle. I'm not here to make money but to spread the gospel.

I'm a real friend of God. My whole life is focused on God and on his kingdom. This verse really encourages me because there's no way that someone can accuse me of being an adulterer.

They can call me a false prophet and a false teacher. They might think that because I teach and do things that are hard for some religious people to accept. But they can't say that I'm a friend of the world. It really doesn't matter what people say against me. What matters is what God thinks of me.

This passage has become one of my life verses. If you read many of my books, you would have seen me repeatedly quote this verse. I don't intend to be heavy on you and cast a yoke around your neck that is too hard to bear. This is about the way that I live my life and the verses that have impacted me. The worst thing you could ever hear are the words, "Depart from me, I never knew you" (Matthew 7:21–23). To my way of thinking, if you become a friend of the world and an enemy of God, this is what you might hear.

Chapter 16

Luke 12:16–21

"Then He spoke a parable to them, saying: 'The ground of a certain rich man yielded plentifully. And he thought within himself, saying, "What shall I do, since I have no room to store my crops?" So he said, "I will do this: I will pull down my barns and build greater, and there I will store all my crops and my goods. And I will say to my soul, 'Soul, you have many goods laid up for many years; take your ease; eat, drink, and be merry.'" But God said to him, "Fool! This night your soul will be required of you; then whose will those things be which you have provided?"

"So is he who lays up treasure for himself, and is not rich toward God."

This passage is talking about a man with a bumper crop. He tears down a little barn and builds bigger barns to store all his crops. Then he says to himself, *I can drink, eat, and be merry because I have all these crops*. Jesus says that he's a fool because he will have his soul taken from him, and his riches will be given to someone else.

Jesus then compares this man to the person who focuses on treasures for himself on earth instead of being rich toward God.

God is confirming our theme here in many passages. He uses James, John, and Jesus to bring out the same message for followers of Jesus. If you have an income and you spend your money on happiness and eating, drinking, and being merry, then you might need to take another look at your priorities and your relationship with God. If you use your income to provide riches, a comfortable living, a prosperous lifestyle, and a good time, you're not serving God the way you should.

I'm trying to be positive here, but I am able to give a third of my income to the Lord even on the small income that I receive from my disability pension. I still find ways to sow into the kingdom of God on a small income. My situation might be a bit unusual as my housing expenses are low. I don't have a vehicle, and I'm not responsible for a family. Even so, I have made it a priority to give to the Lord.

I know that people with larger incomes also invest in the kingdom. Their priorities might be different. God wants us to be rich toward him and his kingdom, not rich toward ourselves and our pleasures.

In a previous chapter, James said that the reason that you don't receive even when you ask to be blessed is because you want to spend it on your pleasures. Here again, Jesus is saying that this man has all this wealth, and he just wanted to kick back and relax and enjoy himself. Jesus said that's not okay.

I live a life that is totally focused on the kingdom of God and on prospering the kingdom. What's different about me is I know who I am. I know what I'm called to do. I know my future, and I know what to do each day. I am continually working on a new book. I am looking for ideas to further teach people about the kingdom of God.

This book might not be one of my most popular books, but it will give people some insight into some really important verses. Why would I spend two thousand dollars to write and publish a book like this? Because I want people to stand on these verses. I want people to invest their time into meditating on these words and getting these scriptures from their minds down into their hearts into their spirits so that these truths will start to manifest in their lives.

These scriptures are meant to transform you. I'm spending some time explaining them and dissecting what they mean to me. I'm spending some time sharing my life and how these verses relate to me just to reinforce what they mean. You won't be able to take anything to heaven. The only thing that you can take to heaven is people. You can help people become saved or develop a more intimate relationship with Jesus by what you said to them and through investing in the kingdom.

You can only take people to heaven. Only two things are worth investing in: helping people develop a more intimate relationship with Jesus and helping people become saved. These are the only two worthwhile things to invest in on earth. That's what Jesus means when he talks about being rich toward God.

Rich toward God means saving people who aren't saved and helping saved people become more productive and closer to Jesus. Everything else will be burned by the fire, but these two things are worth investing your money into. You'll leave all your riches on earth, and your sons and daughters can squander your wealth.

You can invest in people on earth and encourage others, but the only things you can take to heaven are people who are saved by your efforts and those who develop a richer relationship with Jesus because of you.

I implore you to become rich when it comes to God. I implore you to take hold of these scriptures and start to meditate on them. Start to apply them to your life because they can transform you. They can really bless and encourage you. Learn how you can better the kingdom of Jesus, the kingdom of the Father. Learn how you can sow into the kingdom and start to sow today.

Chapter 17

This is the parable of the prodigal son. I'm going to include the parable here for you to read. I suggest that you actually take the time and read through it and don't skip over it. Then, I'll talk about it after you've read it.

Luke 15:11–32

"Then He said: 'A certain man had two sons. And the younger of them said to his father, "Father, give me the portion of goods that falls to me." So he divided to them his livelihood. And not many days after, the younger son gathered all together, journeyed to a far country, and there wasted his possessions with prodigal living. But when he had spent all, there arose a severe famine in that land, and he began to be in want. Then he went and joined himself to a citizen of that country, and he sent him into his fields to feed swine. And he would gladly have filled his stomach with the pods that the swine ate, and no one gave him anything.

"But when he came to himself, he said, "How many of my father's hired servants have bread enough and to spare, and I perish with hunger! I will arise and go to my father, and will say to him, 'Father, I have sinned against heaven and before you, and I am no longer worthy to be called your son. Make me like one of your hired servants.'"

"And he arose and came to his father. But when he was still a great way off, his father saw him and had compassion, and ran and fell on his neck and kissed him. And the son said to him, "Father, I have sinned against heaven and in your sight, and am no longer worthy to be called your son."

"But the father said to his servants, "Bring out the best robe and put it on him, and put a ring on his hand and sandals on his feet. And bring the fatted calf here and kill it, and let us eat and be merry; for this my son was dead and is alive again; he was lost and is found." And they began to be merry.

"Now his older son was in the field. And as he came and drew near to the house, he heard music and dancing. So he called one of the servants and asked what these things meant. And he said to him, "Your brother has come, and because he has received him safe and sound, your father has killed the fatted calf."

"But he was angry and would not go in. Therefore, his father came out and pleaded with him. So he answered and said to his father, "Lo, these many years I have been serving you; I never transgressed your commandment at any time; and yet you never gave me a young goat, that I might make merry with my friends. But as soon as this son of yours came, who has devoured your livelihood with harlots, you killed the fatted calf for him."

"And he said to him, "Son, you are always with me, and all that I have is yours. It was right that we should make merry and be glad, for your brother was dead and is alive again, and was lost and is found."

This parable is about three people: two sons and a father. Sometimes people think only two people are in this story: the two sons. The younger son totally dishonored and disrespected his father and asked for his inheritance before his father died. Essentially he said, "Dad, I want you dead. I don't respect you. I want your money, but I don't want you."

In the Jewish tradition, that son could have almost lost his life because he was so disrespectful. If children were dishonoring to parents, they could be stoned. The Jews would be very offended to even hear that parable. My pastor says that the reason the father ran to his son is so that he could rescue him before the other men stoned him.

The younger son went off and lived the prodigal lifestyle, spending thousands of dollars on drinking, partying, and paying for prostitutes. I essentially lived that kind of life for many years, not so much the partying but sleeping with the prostitutes. Then famine came upon the land, and the son suffered.

The son spent all his money. He finally found a job feeding pigs. Pigs were unclean to the Jewish person, so it was totally disgusting for a Jewish boy to feed pigs. The Jews would have been appalled at this story as this boy would have been unclean at all times and wouldn't have been able to go to the temple. He was just a hot mess.

Then, at last, he comes to his senses, and he runs home. The father sees him from a long distance, which means the father was watching for his son every day. The father took up his pants, gathered his cloak around him, and ran in an undignified manner to hug his dirty son.

That's the story of our Heavenly Father. That's how he acts toward sinners. He just loves us. That's very encouraging to me. For so much of my life, I was living that life of sin. What an encouraging message that the Father would embrace me so lovingly. That's one reason why this is such a meaningful scripture passage to me. I hope that some of you can understand that the Father really loves you despite what you've done.

Then the son came home, and the father put the best shoes on his boy and gave him a new robe. He put a signet ring on him, which stands for authority.

The father then threw a party, but the oldest son had a stinking attitude about the party. He wouldn't come to the festivities and complained that his dad never had a party for him. The older son called the younger son a disgrace and asked why he was being treated so well.

The older son is much like many people in the church. Once a friend of mine showed me a book about the elder son. The book talked about the attitude of this judging, condemning Christian. When my friend gave me the book, I saw that I was now that person—the older brother, that judgmental Christian that was unforgiving of other Christians. I was very legalistic and angry.

I had previously written an article that said the older son would end up in hell with his attitude. Therefore, you can imagine how upset I was when I saw that I had become the older brother. You can learn more about that story in *The Parables of Jesus Made Simple: Updated and Expanded Edition*, which covers that parable in more depth.

This parable means so much to me because I've become all three people in the story. I've lived the life of the prodigal son. I've lived a life of condemning others and judgmental attitudes as the older brother. And now, I've developed the heart of the Father with love and compassion for sinners and for people who are religious, legalistic, judgmental, and stuck in their ways.

You really need to understand this parable. You need to identify which one of these individuals you are. Are you struggling and needing to come back to the Father to receive his love? Are you religious, condemning, judgmental, and stuck in your own ways? You need to change your attitude and come to a place of intimacy and learn a little bit about grace.

The book, *Destined to Reign* by Joseph Prince, will help you learn more about grace.

This parable means a lot to me because I've known throughout my whole life that I was loved even when I was in sin. Jesus made a point of giving three examples of lost items in Luke 15. He shared the parable of the lost sheep, and then he shared the parable of the lost coin. Finally, he shared the parable of the prodigal son. In each parable, you can see that something precious was lost and then found. After they found the lost sheep, they had a party. The woman who found the lost coin also had a party. And the father held a party for the lost son, the prodigal, who came home. That's how Jesus and the Father feel when you return to him. They want to celebrate and throw a party.

There is so much hope in the parable of the prodigal son, hope for all of us. I am so happy that I don't have to feed the pigs any longer. No matter how hard things are, I can be confident that I have a loving Father in heaven who understands me and wants to heal me in every way. When we consider our lives, we have all been lost at some point like the prodigal. But we don't have to stay that way. We can all come home to the welcoming and waiting arms of the Father.

Chapter 18

This chapter is taken from Matthew 25:14–30, the parable of the talents. You can read the following passage. Once again, I encourage you to read it because we'll talk about it and discuss its impact in my life. After you read it, you can read my thoughts.

Matthew 25:14–30

"For the kingdom of heaven is like a man traveling to a far country, who called his own servants and delivered his goods to them. And to one he gave five talents, to another two, and to another one, to each according to his own ability; and immediately he went on a journey. Then he who had received the five talents went and traded with them, and made another five talents. And likewise he who had received two gained two more also. But he who had received one went and dug in the ground, and hid his lord's money. After a long time the lord of those servants came and settled accounts with them.

"So he who had received five talents came and brought five other talents, saying, 'Lord, you delivered to me five talents; look, I have gained five more talents besides them.' His lord said to him, 'Well done, good and faithful servant; you were faithful over a few things, I will make you ruler over many things. Enter into the joy of your lord.' He also who had received two talents came and said, 'Lord, you delivered to me two talents; look, I have gained two more talents besides them.' His lord said to him, 'Well done, good and faithful servant; you have been faithful over a few things, I will make you ruler over many things. Enter into the joy of your lord.'

"Then he who had received the one talent came and said, 'Lord, I knew you to be a hard man, reaping where you have not sown, and gathering where you have not scattered seed. And I was afraid, and went and hid your talent in the ground. Look, there you have what is yours.'

"But his lord answered and said to him, 'You wicked and lazy servant, you knew that I reap where I have not sown, and gather where I have not scattered seed. So you ought to have deposited my money with the bankers, and at my coming I would have received back my own with interest. Therefore take the talent from him, and give it to him who has ten talents.

"'For to everyone who has, more will be given, and he will have abundance; but from him who does not have, even what he has will be taken away. And cast the unprofitable servant into the outer darkness. There will be weeping and gnashing of teeth.'"

This is an important passage to me, and I believe it will be important to you as well.

In this parable, everyone is given talents: five talents, two talents, and one talent, each according to his ability. Immediately, the man went on a journey. First of all, we need to establish what this parable is all about. I share more about this in *The Parables of Jesus Made Simple: Updated and Expanded Edition*. I want to share here that each of us are given talents according to our abilities. For example, someone might have come from a lovely Christian home with rich parents who brought up that child with love and affection. That child was adored, had beautiful siblings, and went to a great college. The person found an excellent job and then went on to Bible college and obtained a degree. He or she had no debt because the parents paid for school. He or she became a successful evangelist or famous preacher. This person is like someone who received five talents.

People are given talents according to their ability. God gives us a measure of his provision according to our ability. He will not expect you to save tens of thousands of people if you don't have the foundation and the capacity to do that.

He also gives certain people two talents and others one talent. Well, we know in the story the person who received the five talents invested that in other businesses and earned another five talents. The master said to him, "Well done, good and faithful servant; you are faithful over a few things, I will make you ruler over many things. Enter into the joy of your lord."

The person who comes back with another five talents was praised for being a good and faithful servant and was then put in charge of many things. Likewise, the person who was given two talents received a reward for investing them and bringing a return.

I like to think that I was only given one talent. But I didn't hide my talent, making the master angry. I was only given a talent, and I'm not a special person with two or five talents.

I firmly believe that I'm the boy with the loaves and fishes. I'm the woman, that sinner, who washed Jesus's feet. I'm the prodigal son. I believe that Jesus can do exceedingly and abundantly above all I ask or think. I believe that I'm the Psalm 1 one man and the Jeremiah 17 man. I believe all these things about myself. But I don't think I was especially gifted.

I see myself with one talent. But rather than giving one talent back, I see myself giving five talents back. I see myself outperforming the person with two talents and five talents. I have made a focused effort in my life to be a star in heaven.

I'm setting myself up to shine in heaven like the verse in Daniel talks about. I'm setting myself up for maximum rewards.

When you compare me to Benny Hinn, Jesus can say, "Well, Matthew had a lot less, and he did very well with what he had. He outperformed you, Benny Hinn and Joyce Meyer. You were given opportunities that Matthew wasn't, and he's outperformed you." I hope that will happen.

I was always encouraged by the story of the tortoise and the hare. The tortoise crawled along while the hare raced off. But the hare thought that winning was a foregone conclusion, so it stopped and became distracted. In the end, the tortoise won the race because it kept going, slow but sure. I see myself more as a tortoise with no special ability. It isn't especially fast or gifted but endures and concentrates on the race and succeeds. This is such an encouraging parable to me.

I don't want to focus on the person with the one talent. But I do want to tell people that if you don't know your life purpose and if you go through life without fulfilling that purpose, what have you accomplished? If you're just going to church but you're not doing what God called you to do, do you think you have invested your talent wisely?

I think that very few in the church invest their talent wisely. I believe that people with two and five talents might not invest their talents either. I believe that so many people were given opportunities for the kingdom but just didn't use them for God. They use their talents to build their own empire and their own name, but they don't use them to build the kingdom. That's a bit of a hard word, but I'm still encouraged by this. I know that I've been given this life on earth, and I've been called to prosper. I'm especially blessed to know this parable.

I hope this has encouraged you. Do you see yourself with one talent, two talents, or five talents? Do you currently know your life purpose? You can read my book, *Finding Your Purpose in Christ*, and discover your purpose. Then, start to practice and apply yourself to that purpose.

Chapter 19

1 John 2:6

"He who says he abides in Him ought himself also to walk just as He walked."

The apostle John walked and taught with Jesus Christ. John is writing here, and he understood who Jesus Christ was. He had a wonderful relationship with Jesus and said in his own words that he was the closest apostle to Jesus. John really understood Jesus. In the Gospel of John, he says three times, "If you love Jesus, you need to obey his commands." He then repeated this three more times in his letters to the churches for a total of six times.

That's an especially important message. John is essentially saying that if you love Jesus, if you say that you abide in him, then you ought to walk like him and behave like him. Others should be able to say to you, "You really remind me of Jesus."

I've been fortunate to hear from different people three times in my life that I'm the most Christ-like person they know. I don't say that to boast. One of the people was my younger brother. He once told his daughter, "Matthew, your uncle, is the most Christ-like person I know." Another friend of the family told my mother that I was the most Christ-like person she knew.

When you start to hear that from time to time, you start to realize that this verse isn't just an important verse to you. You now are beginning to live out this verse. As you understand and meditate on the commands of Jesus for years and start to walk out those commands, you become aligned with the character and the personality of Jesus. It affects everything you do when you start to behave like Jesus.

This will change your attitudes with certain people, change how you behave and react to situations. So many things can distract us and come against us and cause us to react negatively. When you show grace to other people in your reactions, you are showing a practical difference in your life.

This is my forty-second book. I have many people who write negative reviews of my books. They claim my books aren't scriptural or biblical and call my views heresy. They say that I'm a false prophet along with other negative comments. How I behave when I am attacked is important to God. How I react to their words is what counts. This shows the strength of my character; it's not always what I do in public. It's how I treat the person who is getting in my face and causing trouble. It's how I behave in private that really counts. Many people can have a public persona and image. But they might treat their wife and children terribly. We don't know what goes on behind closed doors. People can really suffer because of a family member. I know this personally as my dad used to be a very angry father.

We need to meditate on this verse and understand what John meant here. He wrote the verse because he was behaving like Jesus. John and the other apostles acted like Jesus. When a rabbi taught his students in those days, his students followed him and learned everything he taught. Then, when the rabbi retired or passed on, the students became rabbis with their own students. They were now responsible to teach the next generation.

Jesus was like a rabbi, and he taught others as a rabbi although he didn't have the official title of a rabbi. He taught his students, and they became like him. They could be identified because they acted like him. If you met the apostle John today at dinner or out at a church fellowship, he would remind you of Jesus. You'd think that you were talking to Jesus.

We have to live a life that culminates and comes to a point where we're like Jesus and officially representing him. Don't just live as a Christian, but live as Christ. Become Christ, become the anointed one in your community. Become that tree that's planted by the rivers who is sourced by the water so that it gives fruit in season so that it has leaves that do not wither when the drought comes as Psalm 1 and Jeremiah 17 say.

Become a sustaining tree that can give fruit and holy sustenance to people, that can bless people. You want to provide people with everything that they need. Become love in every situation and respond in love to whatever happens to you. Don't be religious or bound up with a set of rules, but be flexible, relatable, loving, and compassionate in everything you say and do.

Don't wear a mask or wear the face of Christianity. Instead, demonstrate Jesus wherever you go and whatever you do. Do you know Jesus? You can find Jesus through understanding his parables. Read my book, _The Parables of Jesus Made Simple: Updated and Expanded Edition_. You will understand the parables that Jesus taught and start to put his teachings into practice.

When you know and understand Jesus, you can trust and obey him because you understand that he is true, real, right, smart, and wise. The more you obey him, the more you'll realize how smart he is. As you obey him, you become more like him. It's our goal in life to become more like Jesus.

I encourage you to ponder and meditate on this verse. Think about it. It's not impossible to live this out because John did. I'm also living out this verse, and it's possible for you to live it out as well.

Closing Thoughts

I hope that I've achieved a couple of purposes with this book. I hope that I've given you several verses to print out, meditate on, and apply in your own life. I hope that out of the nineteen scriptures, you can pick at least ten of them and start to meditate on them. Start to apply these passages to your life.

My aim is to really encourage people and explain my life verses. I had a twofold goal in this book. I wanted to show you some solid verses that you could learn to live by and apply in your own life. My second goal was to share with you where I'm coming from and how important these verses are to me. I want you to understand how powerful scripture can be in your own life.

I encourage you to look at the fifty commands of Jesus at this link. If you are reading the paperback, you can search for my ezine article on the fifty commands of Jesus. I also encourage you to read *Finding Your Purpose in Christ*. You can benefit from reading all my books. I would certainly love it if you supported my ministry. You can find out more about that on the page at the end of this book, "How to Sponsor a Book Project."

My job in this world is to educate Christians and to teach them how to live the proper Christian life, a successful and prosperous Christian life. My goal is to teach Christians how to do the following:
- prosper,
- be the light of Jesus,
- be a light on the hill,
- prophesy,

- walk in miracles, signs, and wonders,
- live under an open heaven,
- interact with angels, and
- do many things in the kingdom.

You can also see a list of other books that I've written toward the end of this book.

I really encourage you to look through my books and buy ten more of my books on Kindle. Read and apply the books in your life. Print out a list of the verses in this book and pick eight to twelve of them that really apply to you. Put up the printed sheet on your refrigerator, on a wall, or in a picture frame. Read them and soak them in. Apply them and meditate on them over the years so that they become real to you. You will then start to live them out and be blessed by them.

I want to end this simply in a prayer for you now.

Dear Father,

I pray that this reader is powerfully affected by what I've said in this book. I pray that they can review what I've said and seriously contemplate what has been written and start to apply these lessons in their own life. I pray that they won't just read this book and say that it was great. Instead, I pray that they'll print out the verses that apply to them and meditate on and practice those verses. I pray that they will search the scriptures and find other meaningful verses to add to the list and live out and practice those verses as well.

I pray that you would speak to them and encourage them. I pray that your Holy Spirit's anointing would increase in their life and that they would develop an intimacy with you that surpasses any other relationship that they have. Draw close to them and guide them and direct them in everything that they do and say.

In Jesus's name, I ask. Amen.

God bless you and keep you.

I'd love to hear from you

One of the ways that you can bless me as a writer is by writing an honest and candid review of my book on Amazon. I always read the reviews of my books, and I would love to hear what you have to say about this one.

Before I buy a book, I read the reviews first. You can make an informed decision about a book when you have read enough honest reviews from readers. One way to help me sell this book and to give me positive feedback is by writing a review for me. It doesn't cost you a thing but helps me and the future readers of this book enormously.

To read my blog, request a life-coaching session, request your own personal prophecy, or to receive a personal message from your angel, you can also visit my website at http://personal-prophecy-today.com All of the funds raised through my ministry website will go toward the books that I write and self-publish.

To write to me about this book or to share any other thoughts, please feel free to contact me at my personal email address at survivors.sanctuary@gmail.com

You can also friend request me on Facebook at Matthew Robert Payne. Please send me a message if we have no friends in common as a lot of scammers now send me friend requests.

You can also do me a huge favor and share this book on Facebook as a recommended book to read. This will help me and other readers.

How to Sponsor a Book Project

If you have been blessed by this book, you might consider sponsoring a book for me. It normally costs me between fifteen hundred and two thousand dollars or more to produce each book that I write, depending on the length of the book.

If you seek the Holy Spirit about financing a book for me, I know that the Lord would be eternally grateful to you. Consider how much this book has blessed you and then think of hundreds or even thousands of people who would be blessed by a book of mine. As you are probably aware, the vast majority of my books are ninety-nine cents on Kindle, which proves to you that book writing is indeed a ministry for me and not a money-making venture. I would be very happy if you supported me in this.

If you have any questions for me or if you want to know what projects I am currently working on that your money might finance, you can write to me at survivors.sanctuary@gmail.com and ask me for more information. I would be pleased to give you more details about my projects.

You can sow any amount to my ministry by simply sending me money via the PayPal link at this address: http://personal-prophecy-today.com/support-my-ministry/

You can be sure that your support, no matter the amount, will be used for the publishing of helpful Christian books for people to read.

Other Books by Matthew Robert Payne

The Prophetic Supernatural Experience

Prophetic Evangelism Made Simple

Your Identity in Christ

His Redeeming Love: A Memoir

Writing and Self-Publishing Christian Nonfiction

Coping with your Pain and Suffering

Living for Eternity

Jesus Speaking Today

Great Cloud of Witnesses Speak

My Radical Encounters with Angels

Finding Intimacy with Jesus Made Simple

My Radical Encounters with Angels: Book Two

A Beginner's Guide to the Prophetic

Michael Jackson Speaks from Heaven

7 Keys to Intimacy with Jesus

Conversations with God: Book 1

Optimistic Visions of Revelation

Conversations with God: Book 2

Finding Your Purpose in Christ

Influencing your World for Christ: Practical Everyday Evangelism

Deep Calls unto Deep: Answering Questions on the Prophetic

My Visits to the Galactic Council of Heaven

The Parables of Jesus Made Simple: Updated and Expanded Edition

Great Cloud of Witnesses Speak: Old and New

Walking under an Open Heaven

A Message from My Angel: Book 1

Interviews with the Two Witnesses: Enoch and Elijah Speak

Gaining Freedom from Sex Addictions: Breaking Free of Pornography and Prostitutes

Mary Magdalene Speaks from Heaven: A Divine Revelation

Princess Diana Speaks from Heaven: A Divine Revelation

How to Hear God's Voice:
Keys to Conversational Two-Way Prayer

Apostle John Speaks from Heaven: A Divine Revelation

What I Believe

Great Cloud of Witnesses Speak: God's Generals

Apostle Peter Speaks from Heaven: A Divine Revelation

King David Speaks from Heaven: A Divine Revelation

Twenty-Two Signs that You're Called to Be a Prophet

Five Keys to Successful Writing:
How I Write One Book per Month

You can find my published books on my Amazon author page here: http://tinyurl.com/jq3h893

Upcoming Books:
Apostle Paul Speaks from Heaven: A Divine Revelation

About Matthew Robert Payne

Matthew was raised in a Baptist church and was led to the Lord at the tender age of eight. He has experienced some pain and darkness in his life, which have given him a deep compassion and love for all people.

Today, he's a founding member and admin of a Facebook group called "Prophetic Training Group," and he invites you to join him there. Matthew has a commission from the Lord to train up prophets and to mentor others in the Christian faith. He does this through his Facebook posts and by writing relevant books on the Christian faith.

God originally commissioned him to write at least fifty books in his life, but that has now increased to ninety books. He spends his days writing and earning the money to self-publish. You can support him by donating money at http://personal-prophecy-today.com or by requesting any of the other services available through his ministry website.

Recently, the Lord has put it on his heart to start his own publishing company for other people's books to be called Christian Book Publishing USA. It is Matthew's hope to help some people self-publish their books in the future.

It is Matthew's prayer that this book has blessed you, and he hopes it will lead you into a deeper and more intimate relationship with God.

www.ingramcontent.com/pod-product-compliance
Lightning Source LLC
Chambersburg PA
CBHW052109070526
44584CB00017B/2407